Where Are the Eggs?

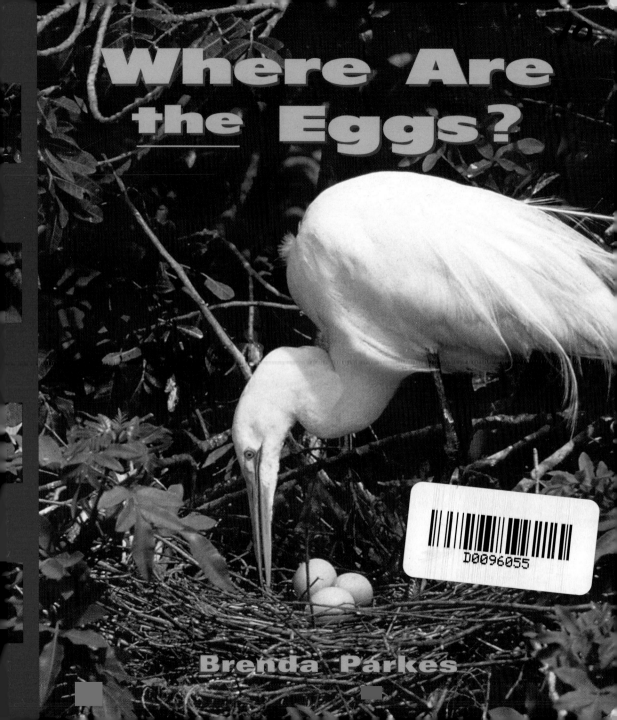

Brenda Parkes

F/9

Where Are the Eggs?
ISBN: 1-56784-521-5

Written by Brenda Parkes
Edited and Designed by Curriculum Concepts

Newbridge Educational Publishing
333 East 38th Street, New York, NY 10016
Copyright © 1999 Newbridge Educational Publishing, LLC

Credits
Cover: James H. Robinson/Animals Animals; Title
Page: Comstock; Page 2: Robert Maier/Animals
Animals; Page 3: Comstock; Page 4: Michael
Husar/DRK Photo; Page 5: Wolfgang Kaehler
Photography; Page 6: Wolfgang Kaehler Photography;
Page 7: Marc Epstein/DRK Photo; Page 8: James
Rod/Photo Researchers, Inc.; Page 9: Mitsuaki
Iwago/Minden Pictures; Page 10: C. C.
Lockwood/DRK Photo; Page 11: Hans Reinhard/
Bruce Coleman, Inc.; Page 12: Hans Pfletschinger/
Peter Arnold, Inc.; Page 13: Johnny Johnson/DRK
Photo; Page 14: Bruno P. Zehnder/Peter Arnold, Inc.;
Page 15: Art Wolfe/Tony Stone Images; Page 16:
Superstock; Back Cover: Marty Cordano/DRK Photo

10 9 8 7 6 5 4

Where Are the Eggs?

Brenda Parkes

Some animals lay eggs.
They lay their eggs
in many different places.

Where will this robin
lay her eggs?

Here they are.
They are in a nest in a tree.

Where will this goose
lay her eggs?

Here they are.
They are in a nest
on the ground.

Where will this alligator
lay her eggs?

Here they are.
They are in a nest
on the ground, too.

Where will this sea turtle
lay her eggs?

Here they are.
They are in a hole
in the sand.

Where will this butterfly
lay her eggs?

They are under a leaf.
When the babies hatch,
they will eat the leaf.

This penguin will lay
her egg on the ice.

Where is the egg now?
The father penguin has it
on his feet.

He keeps the egg warm until
it hatches into a baby penguin.

Parents take care of eggs
so babies hatch and grow.